MW00883411

CS AND THE WAY OF JESUS:
DOM PERSPECTIVE

POLITICS AND WAY OF JES

BY JEREMY TREAT

POLIT
A KIN(

Text co
Design

Special

All righ
reprod
any me
electro
written
brief qu
other n

First Ed

Reality Church of Los An

POLITICS
AND THE WAY
OF JESUS

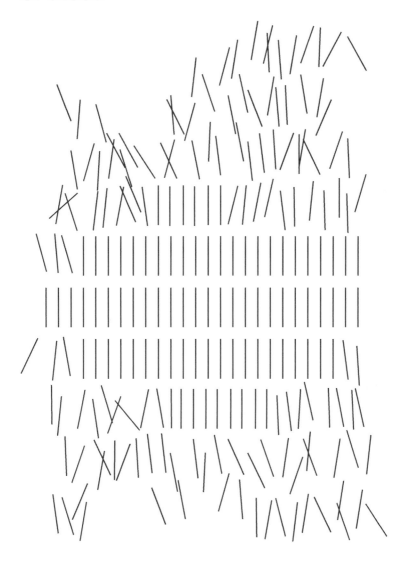

A
KINGDOM
PERSPECTIVE

FOLLOW ME

A SIMPLE GUIDE TO FOLLOWING JESUS

The invitation of Jesus wasn't merely to believe in God or become a religious person. His call was, and still is, "Follow me," an invitation to be with Jesus, learn from Jesus, and become like Jesus. This short book unpacks what it means to follow Jesus and guides Christians down a pathway of discipleship.

GOD'S WILL FOR MY LIFE

A THEOLOGY OF DECISION-MAKING

Life's biggest questions point us to a bigger one: "What is God's will for my life?" We all long for answers, but what does Scripture have to say about the way we make decisions? This short, clear book unpacks what it means to make wise decisions guided by God's Spirit for God's glory.

Contents

INTRODUCTION
IMPORTANT BUT NOT ULTIMATE   07

CHAPTER 1
HOW TO TALK ABOUT POLITICS   13

CHAPTER 2
PROVIDING AN ALTERNATIVE   19

CHAPTER 3
GOD AND GOVERNMENT   25

CHAPTER 4
LOVE IS BETTER   33

CHAPTER 5
PRIDE AND POWER   41

CHAPTER 6
PRAYER, WISDOM, AND CONSCIENCE   49

SUMMARY
TWENTY KEY PRINCIPLES   58

INTRO

Important but Not Ultimate

JESUS IS NOT A REPUBLICAN OR DEMOCRAT. HE'S THE KING OF KING AND LORD OF LORDS.

Politics is tearing our country apart. And you don't have to be a pundit to see it. Whether you're watching the news or scrolling through social media, it's clear that politics has invaded every space and brought with it tension and division.

The 24-hour news cycle pushes the left and right further apart and the widening gap gets filled with mud-throwing, name-calling, venom-spewing rhetoric that only increases the animosity. We see it online: old friends engaged in heated arguments where no one changes their mind and someone ends up unfriended or blocked. Family gatherings have become partisan battlegrounds rather than settings of love, compassion, and empathy.

We're trapped in a political cycle that feels like it's spiraling out of control, with both parties demanding our absolute loyalty to an entire framework of beliefs and policies. Nuance falls by the wayside. It's either in or out, wise or foolish, good or evil. We're told to pick a side and vote accordingly.

HOW SHOULD CHRISTIANS RESPOND?

In this hyper-partisan climate, many followers of Jesus have chosen to withdraw from political engagement altogether. Often turned off by identity politics and corrupt politicians, these Christians relegate their faith to the private realm, focusing simply on their individual relationship with God.

But while some followers of Jesus seek to be apolitical, many others have become all-political. For these Christians, the ultimate problem in the world is a political one and therefore the only solution is a political one, usually as proclaimed by CNN or Fox News.

Fortunately, Scripture shows a better way forward.

In the gospel of Mark, Jesus is confronted by leaders of both the Pharisees and the Herodians—the far right and far left parties of his day. Attempting to trap Jesus, they ask him if taxes should be paid to Caesar. Jesus requests a coin. *Mark 12:16-17* says:

> *And they brought one. And he said to them, "Whose likeness and inscription is this?"*
>
> *They said to him, "Caesar's."*
>
> *Jesus said to them, "Render to Caesar the things that are Caesar's, and to God the things that are God's." And they marveled at him.*

RATHER THAN
SETTLING
FOR BEING
APOLITICAL OR
ALL-POLITICAL,
THE SCRIPTURES
CAST A VISION
OF BEING
APPROPRIATELY
POLITICAL,
WHERE POLITICS
ARE IMPORTANT
BUT NOT
ULTIMATE.

POLITICS ARE IMPORTANT

When Jesus says, "Render to Caesar the things that are Caesar's" he is affirming the God-given place of government in society. This shouldn't be a surprise, since government has always been part of God's good design for creation. And while no government is perfect, it's certainly better than anarchy. We need government to restrain evil and uphold justice. In the United States, for example, without political change there would still be chattel slavery, women would not be allowed to vote, and freedom of religion would not exist.

People often have negative connotations towards politics because they associate politics with partisanship. But we can't reject politics altogether simply because some people have compressed all the world's solutions into one political party. **Jesus was not partisan but he was political**. And while our ultimate allegiance is to God, we still have an obligation to government. Politics are important.

POLITICS ARE NOT ULTIMATE

Politics are good for some things, but our society has tried to make it the answer to everything. Politics has overstepped its bounds and is being asked to solve problems it cannot fix. We end up looking for political solutions to spiritual, relational, and cultural problems.

David Zahl calls politics America's favorite replacement religion, saying, "If once upon a time we looked to politics primarily for governance, we now look to it for belonging, righteousness, meaning, and deliverance—in other words all the things for which we used to rely on Religion."[1] That's why people are placing their ultimate hope in politics. And that's why you need to be aware of the real temptation of being co-opted by a broader political movement, then fitting Jesus into that.

When Jesus says, "Render to Caesar the things that are Caesar's, and to God the things that are God's," he is not minimizing the importance of politics, he is putting it in its place. In other words, **give your taxes to the government**. **Give your allegiance to the kingdom of God**, an allegiance that must overrule your loyalty to a political party.

JESUS IS OUR HOPE

If you give your allegiance to God, you won't fit neatly into either of the two political parties. Jesus is not a Republican. Jesus is not a Democrat. He's the King of Kings and Lord of Lords. He's not lobbying for votes, he's ruling with grace. He's not campaigning for a party, he's building his kingdom.

The question is, who are you putting your ultimate hope in?

What we need is not a privatized faith or a politicized faith, but a holistic faith which acknowledges that politics are important but not ultimate.

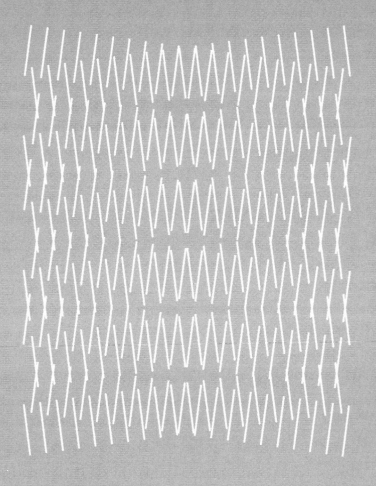

CHAPTER 1

How to Talk About Politics

IMAGINE IF CHRISTIANS WERE KNOWN FOR THEIR LOVE, ESPECIALLY DURING POLITICAL CAMPAIGNS.

People have always disagreed about politics and they always will. After all, we're dealing with complex, nuanced ideas that require much wisdom to apply to everyday life. But what if the problem isn't merely the political ideas about which we differ?

What if the problem (or at least a large part of it) is that we've lost the ability to dialogue with people with whom we disagree?

This is exactly what has happened in our society today. Social media and podcasts transform our opinions into convictions, then offer an assortment of tribalistic communities. With the help of algorithms and online echo chambers, our convictions then become moral absolutes and we distance ourselves from those on "the other side." Whole communities form around our political persuasions and we assume that anyone who doesn't see things the way we do is either evil or an imbecile.

Fortunately, there's a better way forward. **If we approach conversations with tolerance, empathy, and love, we can reshape the political climate around us.**

TOLERANCE

Tolerance is one of the highest virtues in our society today, made clear by the fact "intolerant" is one of the worst names a person can be called. But what do we mean by "tolerance"? The way the word is used commonly today, "tolerance" means that all beliefs are equally valid and you're therefore not allowed to say anyone else is wrong. If you think your belief is "the truth," then you're being intolerant to everyone else.

This approach, however, is vastly different from the traditional understanding of the virtue of tolerance. Historically, tolerance means treating someone with respect even when you disagree with their beliefs. Of course people have different beliefs, especially in the realm of politics. **True tolerance is based not on the equality of ideas but on the equality of people**. It sees the dignity in the person on the other side of the conversation before it sees the position they hold.

Recognizing the dignity in others applies to social media as well. The internet is not a hermetically sealed space where the commands of Christ don't apply. Slander on Instagram is still slander. Being divisive on Facebook is still being divisive. Crude talk online is still crude talk.

If you value relationships as much as you value being right, then your political discussions should mostly take place face to face (video chats and telephone calls are good long-distance options). Don't hide behind memes, tweets, and posts. Make the conversation personal.

EMPATHY

If it sounds hard to have a face-to-face conversation with someone that you're looking down on, guess what?

It is.

While it is fine to disagree with someone's ideas, you can't treat them with dignity if you're looking down on them as a person. We must seek to understand them through their own frame of reference. You need empathy.

It's easy to demonize people on the other side of the aisle when you don't know how they arrived there. That won't change until we are able to ask questions and listen well enough to put ourselves in their position.

If your friend sits on the other end of the political spectrum and the only explanation you have is, "she's just dumb" or "he was brainwashed at college," then you lack empathy and you don't actually know your friend. What's worse, those comments only add to the animosity and cruelty plaguing our political discourse. There is enough of that already. We need empathy.

LOVE

Hatred is one of the most powerful forces in our culture right now. When moral outrage is coupled with the dehumanization of our opponents, there aren't many other options. But the problem is that hate induces a response of hate and leads to a never-ending cycle of animosity.

Think about it: **If you respond to hate with hate then you end up becoming what you hate**.

Martin Luther King Jr. rightly diagnosed the problem and pointed to the remedy:

> *Hate begets hate; violence begets violence; toughness begets a greater toughness. We must meet the forces of hate with the power of love.*[2]

Only love can break the cycle of hate. Of course, Dr. King was drawing from the very Scriptures from which he so often preached:

> *Bless those who persecute you; bless and do not curse them. Rejoice with those who rejoice, weep with those who weep. Live in harmony with one another. Do not be haughty, but associate with the lowly. Never be wise in your own sight. Repay no one evil for evil, but give thought to do what is honorable in the sight of all....Do not be overcome by evil, but overcome evil with good.*
> Romans 12:14-17, 21

Imagine what it would be like if Christians were known for their love, especially during political campaigns.

LOOK TO JESUS

The way we talk about politics is just as important as what we believe about politics. If Christians are going to have a different way of engaging in such difficult topics, we need to keep our eyes fixed on Christ.

It is possible to have firm convictions and be respectful of and loving toward people who disagree with us on political matters. Even more, it's necessary.

CHAPTER 2

Providing an Alternative

WE ARE CALLED TO BE A PECULIAR
PEOPLE SHAPED BY OUR DEVOTION
TO JESUS.

The political landscape of our country is complex, messy, and requires nuance. And yet, while the political need is complicated, it often seems that the solution boils down to simply choosing one of two options: Democrat or Republican. Then, on top of the pressure to pick a side, that party immediately attempts to lay claim to ultimate allegiance in your life, even over your commitment to Christ as king.

It's certainly uncomfortable if you find yourself unable to fully agree with either side and you see inconsistencies between both of them with Scripture. But then you might be in just the right place.

FINDING A NEW CENTER

Tim Keller wrote an article for the *New York Times* about the Christian's place in today's politics. The title summed it up nicely: "How Do Christians Fit into the Two-Party System? They Don't."[3] Part of the problem is that our two political parties offer "package deal ethics," meaning that if you care about one issue then you must then align with that party on all other issues. You're not allowed to think independently about gun rights, abortion, immigration, racism, and taxes. Pick a side.

The problem is, however, that the biblical teachings on each of these issues don't fit neatly into one side or the other. **The kingdom of God cannot be reduced to one political party**. It stands outside of political parties, critiquing every one of them and calling us to unite in Christ alone.

This does not mean, however, that the church merely finds the middle ground between both parties. As Rich Villodas says, "The Church is not to be found at the 'center' of a left/right political world. The Church is to be a species of its own kind, confounding both left and right, and finding its identity from the 'center' of God's life."[4]

The church is not meant to find the perfect place on our existing political spectrum, but rather to offer a different kind of political community altogether.

This also doesn't mean that a Christian can't support a political party. They just need to make sure their allegiance is to the kingdom of God before their political party, and that they can still unite with other Christians who vote differently than they do. The church is our primary community.

A DIFFERENT KIND OF COMMUNITY

Jesus called the church a "city on a hill" *(Matthew 5:14)*. The Greek word he used for city is *polis*, which is where we get the word "politics." **The church, therefore, is an alternative *polis*, a different kind of city where greatness is defined by service, power is guided by love, and justice is truly given for all**. We are different.

We don't have a cancel culture.
We have a forgiveness culture.

We don't respond to hate with hate.
We respond to hate with love.

We don't wag our finger at others.
We repent of our own sins.

We don't demonize our enemies.
We pray for them.

And our quiet faithfulness has a subversive effect on a culture screaming for peace.

This kind of community is exactly what's needed in our culture today. Patrick Deneen, a professor of political science at Notre Dame, argues that, while Conservatives and Liberals are often viewed as polar opposites, they actually have something far greater in common—their rugged individualism.[5] That is why, during this time of division and fragmentation, there is an opportunity for the church to provide the kind of community that we were made for and that the government cannot give us.

The church is the community of the kingdom of God and we are called to be a peculiar people shaped by our devotion to Jesus. No matter who is in the Oval Office, Christ is on the throne. Jesus tore down the dividing wall of hostility and makes us one people and gives us peace. It's through the gospel that we are made citizens of the kingdom, are formed as virtuous people, and become a community that offers a different way of life.

A PEOPLE UNITED BY JESUS

When politics causes division, we must fight for unity in the church. This does not mean we all need to be Democrats, Republicans, third party, or apolitical. That would be uniformity. Christ does not want or expect his church to be uniform. Even Christ's apostles were not united in political beliefs. Matthew was a tax collector working for and benefiting from the Roman occupation of Israel. Simon was a Zealot who wanted a violent end to Roman rule. But they found unity in following Jesus.

This kind of unity is only possible through the gospel and it has been on display throughout church history. Justin Martyr, a follower of Jesus in the second century, put it well when he said, **"We used to hate and destroy one another and refused to associate with people of another race or country. Now, because of Christ, we live together with such people and pray for our enemies."**[6]

WHILE THERE
ARE CERTAINLY
DIFFERENT
POLITICAL
VIEWS IN THE
CHURCH, WHAT
WE HAVE IN
COMMON
IN CHRIST
IS GREATER
THAN OUR
DIFFERENCES
APART FROM
HIM.

3

CHURCH

STATE

CHAPTER 3

God and Government

Government is not a necessary evil, nor is it a human invention designed to rebel against God. **Government was God's idea**. He created it and we need it.

God told Adam and Eve to "fill the earth and subdue it, and have dominion" (*Genesis 1:26*). This is political language, a call to royalty. It's about using God-given power for the purpose of the ordering and flourishing of society. God is king and reigns over all, but he delegates his authority to humans (and to human institutions) to govern his world.

WE NEED GOVERNMENT

From the opening pages of the Bible it's clear that governance is part of God's good design for creation. But we don't live in Eden. Adam and Eve, along with all of humanity, committed treason against God. Every one of us was born into a fallen world where sin has infected every facet of life, including politics. The strong often take advantage of the weak and the powerful oppress those without power. The purpose of government, therefore, is no longer simply to provide order for flourishing, but also to restrain evil and punish injustice.

Of course, no government today perfectly fulfills its purpose. And yet, we still need government. Imagine dialing 911 and having nobody answer. Imagine Los Angeles with no stop lights. Imagine if there were no means to uphold justice or to root out corruption. Anarchy is not a good option.

While the Bible endorses the concept of government, it does not prescribe any particular form of government. It's important that we don't associate Christianity with one specific form of government because the movement of Jesus is made up of a multi-national, multi-ethnic, multi-lingual people. When it comes to government, the only essential unity we have is that we submit to Christ the king. But that does not mean some forms of government aren't better or worse than others. Winston Churchill put it well: "Democracy is the worst form of government, except for all the others."[7]

Being in a democracy creates for us a rather different political situation than that of first-century Christians. Then, and for many Christians in the world today, applying their faith to politics simply meant being faithful to Jesus no matter what the government did, because they didn't have a say in the matter. For Christians in a democracy, we still need to be faithful to Christ under whatever government we're in, but we also have the opportunity to hold accountable and influence the government. But that leaves us with a difficult and important question.

How should the church relate to the state?

Jesus said, "Render to Caesar what belongs to Caesar and to God what belongs to God" (*Matthew 22:21*), describing a clear difference between church and state. But if there's a separation between the two, then how does one relate to the other? The short answer is that church and state are distinct but overlapping.

CHURCH AND STATE ARE DISTINCT

Abraham Kuyper, a Dutch theologian and prime minister of the Netherlands, taught a helpful principle called "sphere sovereignty." The basic idea is that **Jesus reigns over all, but he reigns over different spheres of life in different ways.** For example, he's given parents authority in the home, elders authority in the church, and political rulers authority in the state.[8]

Each area of life has a different purpose and role. The state brings order for flourishing and the restraint of evil. The church proclaims the gospel and makes disciples of Jesus. Church and state, therefore, need to recognize and encourage each other's distinct God-given responsibilities. Each must rule in its own jurisdiction. It is not the state's job to preach the word. It is not the church's responsibility to write laws and policies. A murderer who comes to faith in Jesus can be forgiven of all his sins in the church, but that doesn't mean he will not be held accountable by the state for his actions.

It is critical that the state remains neutral outside its jurisdiction. For example, the state should not force a single religion on its citizens, nor should it allow persecution based on religion. As Christians, we believe the gospel must be freely proclaimed and freely received. If we Christians want the freedom to express our faith, then we must stand up for the religious freedom of other faiths as well, including Islam, Judaism, Hinduism, Buddhism, and all other religions.

CHURCH AND STATE ARE OVERLAPPING

But the separation of church and state is not as easy as saying, "You stay in your lane, I'll stay in my lane, and everything will be fine." We're all on the same freeway together and the lanes inevitably cross. There is a separation of the *institutions* of church and state, but in daily life they operate in the same contested spaces and there is no place of neutrality.

The state is not the church and it should not seek to replace or supplant the church, yet it cannot exist in a purely neutral religious place. For example, laws against murder were founded on religious beliefs about the value of human life.

The church is not the state, but is inescapably political. We are an embassy of the kingdom of God on earth and the goal of our communal life is to witness to Christ the king. **Our faith is personal but it is not private**. Our public faith shapes all of life and is based on the declaration that the turning point of human history was not the

Enlightenment or the founding of the United States, but the death and resurrection of a Nazarene carpenter outside Jerusalem.

As an organization, the church must maintain a clear separation from the state. A pastor should not tell the congregation who to vote for, nor should he bring candidates before the church for the sake of endorsement.

But as an organism, the people of the church are trained and sent out to speak truth to the state and to be salt and light in the political realm. **Separation of church and state does not mean there should be a separation between one's faith and politics**.

THE GOVERNMENT SHALL REST ON HIS SHOULDERS

In *Isaiah 9*, Israel is in a difficult political situation, under attack by the surrounding nations. And it's within that context that the Lord makes a promise:

> *For to us a child is born, to us a son is given; and the government shall be upon his shoulders. (v. 6)*

Jesus brings a kingdom that is like no other kingdom of this world.

Earthly governments are temporary.
The kingdom of Christ is eternal.

Earthly governments are flawed.
The kingdom of Christ is perfect.

Earthly governments are corrupted by injustice.
The kingdom of Christ is founded on perfect justice.

Earthly governments can at best restrain evil.
The kingdom of Christ will abolish evil and
establish peace.

OUR FAITH IS PERSONAL BUT IT IS NOT PRIVATE.

CHAPTER 4

Love Is Better

THE GOVERNMENT CAN'T CHANGE THE HEART, BUT LOVE CAN.

In our politically tense world, we must look to God's word for perspective and guidance. *Romans 13* is one of the key passages in Scripture on politics, and while it's deep and complex, there are three simple points that can be drawn from it for our context today: leaders are necessary, laws are good, and love is better.

LEADERS ARE NECESSARY

Romans 13:1 makes a bold claim, "Let every person be subject to the governing authorities. For there is no authority except from God, and those that exist have been instituted by God." In an age of corrupt politicians, this command feels strange. Are we really called to submit to government leaders, even when they're driven by greed and partisan gain?

Affirming God's sovereignty over governing authorities and the call for Christians to submit to them does not mean those authorities won't be held accountable for their actions or that we owe unconditional obedience to them. The point is that all human authority is derived from God's authority. And since it comes from God, the authority of government leaders is a delegated authority, not an absolute authority.

Of course, this does not mean that God endorses everything done by a political leader. God-given authority can be misused and abused. Like Jesus said to Pilate before the crucifixion, "You would have no authority over me at all unless it had been given you from above" *(John 19:11)*. Pilate misused his authority to condemn and kill Jesus, yet the authority he used to do this was delegated to him by God.

The apostle Peter could write "Honor the emperor" *(1 Peter 2:17)*, even though the emperor at the time was a psychopath named Nero who terrorized Christians and eventually killed Peter himself. Submitting to the authorities that God has established is about respecting the function of the office, not the character of the one in the office.

For this reason, while it is fine to disagree with a political ruler, Christians are called to do so with respect and love, acknowledging the image of God in that political leader even as we hold them accountable to their God-given authority.

Leaders are always flawed, yet they are an essential part of God's design for government.

LAWS ARE GOOD

Government leaders are called to create and uphold laws that protect people's basic rights and create space for their flourishing. And we can all agree, in general, that laws are good. It's good that ten-year-olds can't drive. It's to everyone's benefit that stealing is not allowed. But while laws are meant to be good, we have to acknowledge two important qualifications to how Christians relate to the laws of their land.

First, we must recognize the distinction between biblical principles and government policies. For Christians, our biblical principles must shape the way we approach government policies. But we cannot confuse the two. The Bible does not give us policies on international trade, carbon dioxide emissions, or public education. If we don't recognize this difference, there is a danger of reading our own policy preferences into Scripture and then claiming to have the only position that's biblical.

Take immigration, for example. Scripture gives clear principles about God's heart for the immigrant and how God's people are to love the immigrant. *Deuteronomy 10:18-19* says the Lord "loves the foreigner residing among you, giving them food and clothing. And you are to love those who are foreigners, for you yourselves were foreigners in Egypt." However, while this biblical principle regarding love for the immigrant is clear, Scripture does not prescribe policies regarding how many immigrants should be allowed in a country or how long visas should last. **Biblical principles must inform our approach to government policies**.

Second, while laws are good, there is certainly a time for Christians to resist the laws of the land. In fact, Christians are obligated to resist the law when the government

forbids what God commands or commands what
God forbids.

Scripture is filled with examples of God's people resisting
the government. The Egyptian Pharaoh ordered Hebrew
midwives to kill newborn boys, but the women refused
to obey. The Babylonian king Nebuchadnezzar issued an
edict that his subjects must bow down and worship his
golden image but three Israelites—Shadrach, Meshach,
and Abednego—resisted. When the Persian king Darius
made a decree that for thirty days nobody could pray "to
any god or man" except himself, Daniel refused.

In *Acts 4:19*, the governing authorities commanded the
apostles to stop preaching the gospel but they replied,
"We cannot help but speak about what we've seen and
heard," and in *Acts 5:29*, they say, "We must obey God
rather than man."

**We have an obligation to the government but our ultimate
allegiance is to God.** When Christians *do* resist the
government, however, they must do so not in violence
but in peace, driven not by hate but by love, and aiming
not for conquest but reconciliation.

LOVE IS BETTER

While many people look to *Romans 13:1-7* for principles
about government, they often miss its connection to
the next three verses (8-10), which are about love.
Immediately after discussing leaders and laws, the Apostle
Paul says, "You shall love your neighbor as yourself," for
"love is the fulfilling of the law."

WE HAVE AN OBLIGATION TO THE GOVERNMENT BUT OUR ULTIMATE ALLEGIANCE IS TO GOD.

We must remember that while Scripture speaks to the legitimacy of government, it also makes clear the limits of government.

The government can't change the heart, but love can. Politicians can't make you a new person, but love can. Laws can't give purpose to your life, but love can.

This is not to minimize legislation: it's important. But you can't legislate internal transformation. The people of God are called to be a people of love:

> *Put on then, as God's chosen ones, holy and beloved, compassionate hearts, kindness, humility, meekness, and patience, bearing with one another and, if one has a complaint against another, forgiving each other; as the Lord has forgiven you, so you also must forgive. And above all these put on love, which binds everything together in perfect harmony.*
> *Colossians 3:12-14*

Love is the social glue of the community of Christ. We are bound together by love for one another and for our city.

Leaders are necessary. Laws are good. Love is better.

5

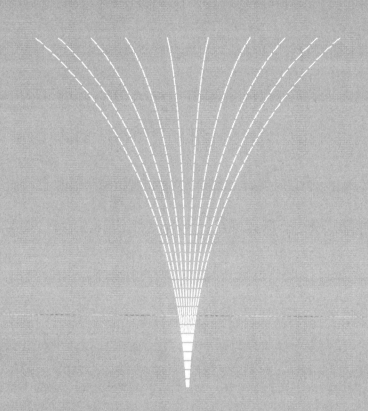

Pride and Power

WORLDLY POWER IS USED FOR SELFISH AMBITION. KINGDOM POWER IS USED FOR SACRIFICIAL LOVE.

The most political statement a Christian can make is "Jesus is Lord." While that may sound like a spiritual utterance to modern ears, first-century Christians lived in a world where the norm was to declare "Caesar is Lord." A commitment to following Jesus, therefore, represented a transformation, not only in followers' hearts but also in the way they related to the political realm around them.

How, then, can Christians today live under the lordship of Jesus while also seeking the good of our cities and nations? We must pledge allegiance to Christ the king while also being aware of the temptation of national pride and the allure of political power.

THE TEMPTATION OF NATIONAL PRIDE

I've travelled the world enough to know the United States is a great place to live. And it's not just the luxuries of paved roads and stop lights. Our country truly has more freedom and opportunity than most civilizations that

WE MUST
PLEDGE
ALLEGIANCE
TO CHRIST THE
KING WHILE
ALSO BEING
AWARE OF THE
TEMPTATION
OF NATIONAL
PRIDE AND
THE ALLURE
OF POLITICAL
POWER.

have existed in the history of our planet. But because there is much good about the U.S., there is a danger of making an idol out of it.

Idolatry is making a good thing an ultimate thing. People often make idols of money, sex, career, and image. It's also possible to make an idol of a nation and for patriotism to become nationalism.

Sadly, this type of national and ethnic idolatry has been all too present in our country. Many Christians see the U.S. as "God's chosen people" and the new Promised Land. But we must remember that **we are citizens of the kingdom of God before we are citizens of the United States of America.**

Russell Moore says, "National identity is important but transitory. There will come a day...when the new republic succumbs to a new creation. We must not shirk from our calling as citizens, but we also must not see our citizenship of the moment as the final word. We are Americans best when we are not Americans first."[9]

Jesus is Lord and our allegiance to him must shape (and override, when necessary) our loyalty to our nation. There is much to be grateful for about our country, but may we never forget this important truth: **the mission of the church is not to make a Christian nation but to make disciples of all nations.**

THE ALLURE OF POLITICAL POWER

Power is the currency of politics in our country today.

And Christians must beware the allure of using political power to accomplish the church's purposes.

History demonstrates that this is a temptation on both sides of the political aisle. In the 1930s, liberal-minded Christians began preaching a "social gospel" that redefined the message of the gospel to what we can do for the world (rather than what God has accomplished in Christ) and often sought political means for their social goals.

This liberal movement, coupled with the sexual revolution of the 1960s, led to a conservative reaction in the church that sought to "take back America," also through political means. The Moral Majority, as the movement become known, tried to accomplish moral goals by wielding political power. It often promoted a gospel-less Christianity that focused on family values and select virtues that advantaged people like themselves while ignoring other biblical virtues that would've benefited people different from them.

For both liberals and conservatives, the ends justified the means and the influence of the church was leveraged for political agendas, resulting in what could be called a prostitution of power. The church became a voting bloc, a demographic to be pulled to the left or right instead of what it should be, a different species altogether that defies cultural categories because our allegiance is to Christ the king.

THE SURPRISING KINGDOM OF CHRIST

Jesus addressed power and pride one day as he was walking with his disciples. James and John had pride that led to a desire for power, and they asked Jesus if they could sit at his right and left in glory. **Jesus doesn't rebuke their desire for power, however, because power is not bad in and of itself. Instead, he redefines greatness by service.** Jesus says, "You know that those who are considered rulers of the Gentiles lord it over them, and their great ones exercise authority over them. But it shall not be so among you....whoever would be great among you must be your servant" *(Mark 10:42-45)*.

Jesus reveals that power in the kingdom is different than power in the world:

Worldly power is used for selfish ambition.
Kingdom power is used for sacrificial love.

Worldly power exploits the weakness of others.
Kingdom power protects the weakness of others.

Worldly power is self-seeking.
Kingdom power is self-denying.

Worldly power is used to suppress.
Kingdom power is used to serve.

Worldly power is about building up ourselves.
Kingdom power is about laying ourselves down for others.

Jesus paints a picture of the kingdom of God where power is used to bless and serve others. And he said all of this on his way to the cross, where Jesus displayed greater power than this world has ever seen—the power of the gospel.

6

Prayer, Wisdom, and Conscience

THERE IS A LOT OF GRAY SPACE IN POLITICS. HOW CAN WE KNOW WHAT TO DO AND FOR WHOM TO VOTE?

The kingship of Jesus completely reorients the way his followers live in our political age. But how does this play out practically? How can we know what to do, who to vote for, and how to relate to people with whom we disagree? For Christians to be faithful to Christ in this cultural moment, we need prayer, wisdom, and a biblical understanding of conscience.

PRAYER IS POLITICAL ACTION

We often engage with politics by reading the news, scrolling through social media, or discussing policies with friends. But while there are many such ways we can engage in politics, there is one thing we *must* do: pray. **Prayer is a political act because it is an appeal to the King of Kings who has all authority and power.** In fact, praying for government officials shows up in Scripture, not as a suggestion, but as a command *(1 Timothy 2:1-2)*.

PRAYER IS A POLITICAL ACT BECAUSE IT IS AN APPEAL TO THE KING OF KINGS WHO HAS ALL AUTHORITY AND POWER.

Why do we spend so little time praying for politics? It may be that, deep down, we believe there is more power in politics than there is in prayer. If we want to see change we assume the best use of our time is to skip over "spiritual matters" and engage in political action. Of course, we should never pit prayer and politics against each other. We must engage politically, but we ought to begin (and continue throughout the process) by appealing to the one whose power is unmatchable and who governs all of human history.

We need to pray for our leaders at all levels of government. Pray for the president and vice president. Pray for your senators and congressional leaders. Pray for your governor, mayor, and local council members. And pray for the church, that we would be faithful to Christ the king and therefore offer a different kind of community than our city is used to seeing.

A Christian's primary political engagement, regardless of who's in office, should be prayer. But along with prayer, we also need wisdom.

WISDOM FOR OUR POLITICAL AGE

In areas of life that are black and white, God gave us laws: do not murder, do not steal, do not cheat on your spouse. But in the gray areas of life, God gives us wisdom. And the majority of life's situations are in the gray areas where moral rules don't provide clear answers. Should you take this job or that job? Which school should you attend? Which apartment should you rent?

There is a lot of gray space in politics. Who should you vote for? Which issues matter the most and how do they relate to one another? What do you do when you agree with a candidate on a very important issue but disagree with that same candidate on several other issues? The Bible doesn't give direct answers to these questions, even though they are all incredibly important. Instead of direct answers, God wants to give us wisdom.

Wisdom is the practical skill to know what to do when the moral commands of Scripture don't clearly apply to a situation. And when it comes to politics, we need wisdom as much as we need oxygen. That's why king Solomon (a political ruler), when he had the chance to ask God for anything in the world, chose wisdom (*1 Kings 3:5-9*). There are three key areas where we need wisdom in politics.

First, we need wisdom to know whom to listen to and trust. Media voices pressure us to pick a side and then view those on the other side as evil or corrupt. We then remove all differing views from our life, creating an echo chamber where we only hear what we already believe. Instead, we need wisdom to know whom to listen to (ideally from multiple perspectives and platforms) and mature believers to guide us through difficult issues.

Second, we need wisdom to know when and where to engage. Far too many people seem to think social media comment threads are the best place to talk about nuanced, personal topics. To know whether it's wise to engage in a discussion or not we should ask, "Is this the right time or place to have a political conversation? Is there a good chance this conversation will be fruitful? Can I keep my cool in this conversation?"

Finally, we need wisdom regarding whom to vote for. The Bible won't tell you a specific person to vote for, but it will give you wisdom and principles that can guide your process. In 1774, John Wesley offered some helpful wisdom on voting:

> I met those of our society who had votes in the ensuing election, and advised them:
>
> 1. To vote, without fee or reward, for the person they judged most worthy.
>
> 2. To speak no evil of the person they voted against, and
>
> 3. To take care their spirits were not sharpened against those that voted on the other side.[10]

A BIBLICAL VIEW OF CONSCIENCE

For a follower of Jesus to engage in politics today, it takes prayer, wisdom, and, finally, a biblical understanding of the conscience.

The conscience is like an internal warning system, giving a sense of what's right or wrong when our mind may not be clear about it. Joe Carter provides a more technical definition: "Our conscience is a part of our God-given internal faculties, a critical inner awareness that bears witness to the norms and values we recognize when determining right or wrong."[11]

While all Christians must submit to the authority of Scripture, there are areas where Christians' consciences will be bound in different ways. Take, for example, alcohol. The Bible is clear that getting drunk is a sin but it does not condemn drinking alcohol in moderation. Therefore, many Christians choose to drink alcohol in moderation. However, there are also many Christians who choose to abstain from alcohol because of their conscience. There is neither a "right" or "wrong" side of the issue, but rather freedom for Christians to act based on their conscience within the bounds of Scripture.

The same principle applies to politics and particularly to voting. All must submit to Scripture. But some may feel in their conscience to vote one way whereas others feel in their conscience to vote another way. There is room for both because we are not bound to other people's consciences.

In short, vote your conscience. But make sure your conscience is chastened by Scripture.

A POLITICAL PRAYER

Father, we humbly ask that our political conversations will be filled with love, our political imaginations will be shaped by Scripture, our political lives will be demonstrations of an alternative way to live, our political understanding of power will always be shaped by Jesus' sacrificial service and that, even as we take our obligation to government seriously, our ultimate political allegiance will always be to your kingdom. We pray for godly wisdom to know whom to listen to and trust, when and where to engage, and whom to vote for. Your kingdom come, your will be done, on earth as it is in heaven. In Christ, by your Spirit, amen.

SUMMARY

Twenty Key Principles

Politics are important,
but not ultimate.

Jesus was not partisan
but he was political.

The way we talk about politics is just as important as what we believe about politics.

If we approach conversations with tolerance, empathy, and love, we can reshape the political climate around us.

If you respond to
hate with hate then
you end up becoming
what you hate.

The kingdom of God cannot be reduced to one political party.

The church is not meant to find the perfect place on our existing political spectrum, but rather to offer a different kind of political community altogether, where greatness is defined by service, power is guided by love, and justice is truly given for all.

Because of Christ, we share life with people different than us and pray for our enemies.

Our faith is personal but it is not private.

Separation of church and state does not mean there should be a separation between one's faith and politics.

We are citizens of
the kingdom of
God before we are
citizens of the United
States of America.

Leaders are always flawed, yet they are an essential part of God's design for government.

Biblical principles
must inform
our approach to
government policies.

Love is the social glue
of the community
of Christ.

The mission of the church is not to make a Christian nation but to make disciples of all nations.

Christians must beware the allure of using political power to accomplish the church's purposes.

Jesus reveals that power in the kingdom is different than power in the world— it loves sacrificially, protects the weakness of others, denies self, serves, and lays itself down for others.

SUMMARY

Prayer is a political act
because it is an appeal
to the King of Kings
who has all authority
and power.

Because there is a lot of gray space in politics, we need wisdom, the practical skill to know what to do when the moral commands of Scripture don't clearly apply to a situation.

Vote your conscience but make sure your conscience is chastened by Scripture.

1. David Zahl, Seculosity: *How Career, Parenting, Technology, Food, Politics and Romance Became Our New Religion and What to Do About It* (Broadleaf Books, 2019)
2. Martin Luther King, Jr., in "Struggle for Equality: Quotes From Martin Luther King, Jr." (*Scholastic Newstime*, 2018)
3. Timothy Keller, "How Do Christians Fit Into the Two-Party System? They Don't," in *The New York Times* (September 29, 2018)
4. Rich Villodas, "An Alternative Community," (sermon, New Life Fellowship, Elmhurst, NY, November 11, 2020)
5. Patrick J. Deenan. *Why Liberalism Failed* (Yale University Press, 2018)
6. Justin Martyr, "The First Apology of Justin, Early Christian Writings, http://earlychristianwritings.com/text/ justinmartyr-firstapology.html (accessed August, 2024)
7. Winston Churchill, "Parliament Bill," (speech, quoting an unsourced aphorism, House of Commons, London, UK, November 11, 1947)
8. Abraham Kuyper "Sphere Sovereignty," in *Sphere Sovereignty: Church, State, Family, Education, and Business*, translated by George Kamp (Monergism, 2024)
9. Russell Moore, *Onward: Engaging the Culture without Losing the Gospel* (B&H Books, 2015)
10. John Wesley, *The Journal of John Wesley* (Waymark, Books 2023)
11. "What Is Conscience?" by Joe Carter, on thegospelcoalition. org, March 4, 2014